Devotional:

Biblical Strategies for a Victorious Life

By Lynette Anderson

Table of Contents

Dedication

I dedicate this devotional to all the warriors. Remember, our worship wins the battle.

After consulting the people, Jehoshaphat appointed men to sing to the Lord and to praise him for the splendor of his[a] holiness as they went out at the head of the army, saying:

"Give thanks to the Lord, for his love endures forever."

22 As they began to sing and praise, the Lord set ambushes against the men of Ammon and Moab and Mount Seir who were invading Judah, and they were defeated. (NIV)

Battling Fear and/or Anxiety

Whoever dwells in the shelter of the Most-High will rest in the shadow of the Almighty. I will say of the Lord, "He is my refuge and my fortress...
Psalm 91: 1-2 (NKJV)

Doubt and worry breed fear! So, in order to eliminate the notion of being afraid we must always know God is with us! Thus, believing He will not forsake us! I have battled anxiety for years, and I have found solace in arresting my fears with songs. Sing this melody with me: "We don't have to worry, doubt, or have fear because the Lord our God is right here!"

My anxiety started in 2010, after the birth of my son. One week after Kaden was born, while visiting my mother, I noticed my feet were swollen and I had a terrible headache. I told my mother I didn't feel "right" but she assured me that I just had a mild case of "baby blues." However, I knew something was wrong. So, I drove to a nearby urgent care clinic. Unfortunately, they were unable to diagnose the cause of my excruciating pain and I was transported to the ER via ambulance.

I was 24-years-old at the time and I didn't know what was going on. What happened next was completely unexpected! The ER nurse checked my vitals and my blood pressure was 200/110, I was rushed to be treated immediately. I pleaded with them to help me before I lost consciousness.

I woke up to the sound of my mother's crying and I realized that I was hooked up to several monitors. My mother told me I suffered a massive seizure and subarachnoid [brain] hemorrhaging. I was in the ICU, and my life hung between time and eternity... death desired me, but God had already established His plan for me! I was eventually diagnosed with eclampsia, a life-threatening condition of seizures that occur shortly after giving birth.

From this experience my battle with anxiety and panic attacks persisted for quite some time. Gratefully, God connected me with Abiding Faith Christian Church; and my pastor guided me through a journey of spiritual relief and deliverance. Now, I know how to call on the name of Jesus. Although my life hasn't been a cake walk, I can face my daily battles with the blessed assurance of knowing I am more than a conqueror; because

Christ overcame ALL things on the cross; thus, HE already won EVERY battle for you and me!

Battling Negative Self-Talk

*You will keep in perfect peace all who trust in
You, all whose thought are fixed on You!"*
Isaiah 26: 2 (NLT)

The commotion of negative thoughts bombards our mind daily. We wrestle with embracing our God-given identity and internalize false perceptions that yield unbeneficial outcomes. We are not validated by what other people may think or say about us; but we are living and breathing masterpieces of our Creator.

So, we must dismiss and cast down feelings of inadequacy, self-hate, and self-doubt. When we do this, we allow God's pre-ordained purpose for our lives to reign and rain because we adjusted our way of thinking. As we see ourselves the way that God sees us, the blinding thoughts of negativity are replaced with the truth of God's word. This practice produces peace and quiets the internal chatter and allows us to win this daily battle.

Battling the Urge of Self-Comparison

"Pay careful attention to your own work, for then you will get the satisfaction of a job well done, and you won't need to compare yourself to anyone else."
Galatians 6:4 (NLT)

Don't fall into the trap of measuring your self-worth, accomplishments, or your personal distance in life to someone else! Comparing ourselves to others diminishes who we are and causes us to go through useless narrations of "coulda, woulda, shouldas!" The only comparisons we should make daily - is the comparison of "US vs. A Better US!"

The most important factor in bettering ourselves is realizing that our growth and improvement is not validated by what someone else has done. Our lives are authored by God, and he knows every turn, setback, advancement, pitfall, and purposeful progressions we will make. Understand this, EVERYONE presents the story that they want others to read... whether it is truth, lies, or deceptively embellished - we are not invited to the calamities behind the scenes.

Fortunately, when we realize that our "true" audience only consists of two individuals—ourselves and God— the burden of measuring up to unattainable goals or reaching untimely pursuits is no longer an issue! We were created to glorify God and our lives are a testament of His goodness, not our works, achievements, or thousands of followers on social media. The urge to compare is highly likely. Please resist the urge and remain focused!

Battling Thoughts of Defeat

"Stand firm against him and be strong in your faith. Remember that your family of believers all over the world is going through the same kind of suffering you are."
I Peter 5:9 (NLT)

How often have we given up too easily, and later regretted it? How many times have we told God NO, when our answer should have been yes? In times when our fight should have been relentless, how many of us have chosen to retreat? Choosing defeat is and will always be a decision that leads to unwanted outcomes.

God's word has instructed us to *trust* Him, in ALL things! The enemy's tactics are a mirage of defeat because God has already DECLARED that we are victors. God's word, His promises, and His plan for our lives is established in heaven and it must manifest on earth; or God would be a liar and it is *totally* IMPOSSIBLE!

Profess this with me: I will stand. I won't give up. I will continue to fight! God's greatness is within me and I have the ability to remain on course and I will emerge from the battle victoriously because God is my fortress.

Battling the Cycles of Temptation

"Watch and pray, that ye enter not into temptation: the spirit indeed is willing, but the flesh is weak." Matthew 26:41 (KJV)

We are innately weak because of the things we inherently desire. Consequently, when we are tempted [continuously], it is always what we want. We can't be tempted by anything that is unappealing to us. Therefore, when we are tempted, it is our faith in God that is tested and not our "seeming" righteousness... remember our purity is as filthy rags to Him.

Since becoming a "follower of Christ" I have fallen, short, more times than I care to admit. My desire to be married superseded my willingness to wait on God. Therefore, I compromised my faith, lowered my standards, and gave into my own lusts for the sake of personal satisfaction. My contentment was temporary, and my regret was instant. Although my repentance was sincere the cycling caused a rift, and my intimacy with God was disturbed.

We overcome temptation with obedience to God. It is impossible to please Him when we try to satisfy our flesh. We must practice self-control and learn to be content with our "now..." until God gives us our future as the present.

Battling the Inevitable

"Cast all your cares upon him; for he careth for you." 1 Peter 5:7 *(KJV)*

Life has suffering. Life is painful. Life has unexpected trials; and life is the unavoidable battlefield everyone must fight through! However, we can take peace in knowing God is with us in the midst of every battle and He delights in our willingness to rely on Him.

When we establish a personal relationship with God, we can go to Him with every burden, worry, care, frustration—everything. God never intended for us to possess the strength to handle everything, if this were the case, we would have no need for Him. "Cast all your cares upon him; for he careth for you." 1 Peter 5:7 KJV So, no matter what battles we face God can take care of it; nothing is too difficult for Him!

Although, we will endure uncertainties and calamities, we are NOT defeated! The Word of God states in John 16:33 (KJV), "These things I have spoken unto you, that in me ye might have peace. In the world ye shall have tribulation: but be of good cheer; I have overcome the world." God has told us we have no need to fret about anything in our lives because He has everything under control.

Battling for Deliverance

"I don't really understand myself, for I want to do what is right, but I don't do it. Instead, I do what I hate."
Romans 7:15 (NLT)

I battle with the same sin! I trip, I fall, I stumble, and at times I have willingly walked directly into my selfish desires (and, again, later regretted it). I want to do better, but more importantly, I want to be better. I have spent countless days and nights beating myself up because my deliverance has NOT been a picture of perfection, but the reality of my own sinful human nature.

I questioned, "Why is it so hard to do the *right* thing? I know my actions are displeasing to God!" In prayer, I realized my continual sinning (iniquity) was my attempt to fill a void. Unfortunately, the sin (my sins) only intensified the void! I now understand, we cannot fill the voids in our lives with things or people, because the space is reserved for our first love– God.

All of us are imperfect, and God knows this and because of this He sent His son Jesus to die for our iniquities. So, I have learned to always confess my sins to God, and I will continue fighting for my deliverance. I also I understand that my deliverance is NOT a one and done task, but it is the working of my faith to prove that God is a keeper of those who desire to be kept! Thus, we should not feel as though we cannot overcome our struggles; we must trust that God will strengthen us to be victorious and not to be consumed by temptation. The lessons are the blessings [when we learn from them].

Battling Feelings of Unworthiness

And I know that nothing good lives in me, that is, in my sinful nature. I want to do what is right, but I can't. I want to do what is good, but I don't. I don't want to do what is wrong, but I do it anyway. But if I do what I don't want to do, I am not really the one doing wrong; it is sin living in me that does it. I have discovered this principle of life—that when I want to do what is right, I inevitably do what is wrong. I love God's law with all my heart. But there is another power within me that is at war with my mind. This power makes me a slave to the sin that is still within me. Oh,

*what a miserable person I am! Who will
free me from this life that is dominated by
sin and death? Thank God! The answer is
in Jesus Christ our Lord. So, you see how
it is: In my mind I really want to obey
God's law, but because of my sinful nature
I am a slave to sin."*
Romans 7:17-25 (NLT)

As human beings we are flawed and fallible and because of this, we constantly question God's grace, mercy, and love towards us. God's love for us is not contingent upon what we do, but His love is solely based on who He is! God knew everything about us before we were formed in our mother's womb. He knew our struggles, weaknesses, and every imperfection. More importantly, God understands our humanness and He knows that we desire to please Him; and despite our inability to "get it right" all the time, God *still* deems us worthy!

Note: I'm not saying it's okay to live in sin, because the wages of sin is death. Simply understand, God knows our struggles. However, He requires sincere repentance, changed actions, and consistent strides to be righteous.

Battling the Effects of Rejection

"So be strong and courageous! Do not be afraid and do not panic before them. For the Lord, your God will personally go ahead of you. He will neither fail you nor abandon you.""

Deuteronomy 31:6 (NLT)

Everyone has dealt with rejection; it is hurtful! Whether the rejection was experienced at work, in a relationship, a "failed" audition, or denied admission into a college or technical program—rejection sends us into an emotional frenzy!

But I've learned that all rejection isn't bad, sometimes rejection is God's way of saying "not yet." We must understand that the right thing at the wrong time is unbeneficial. God gets no glory when the timing is off... everything must align with God's perfect will.

Most of the rejection I've experienced has been within relationships. I have not been in a relationship that lasted longer than a year. Even when I got married the first time, the marriage only lasted eight months. Rejection and unfaithfulness shattered my heart. I spent numerous nights crying because I felt something was wrong *with me*. It seemed as though no man wanted me or loved me *for me*. These relationships scarred me, but I still felt I needed a man *to be* happy! Unfortunately, I compromised frequently because the sex was good, they had my mind but for me they didn't have time. To this end, I experienced rejection repeatedly.

Thankfully, I've come to a place of valuing me, respecting me, and loving me! I know *"who I am"* and *"whose I am."* I am one of God's distinct masterpieces and I know He wants the best for me! So, I make conscious efforts to obey God's word and will for my life; and if I fall, I repent sincerely because I know God will forgive me. I believe God's plan for my life is unimaginably spectacular; so, I encourage every reader to embrace and accept God's love for you! He will never leave or forsake us.

Battling Loneliness

"As one whom his mother comforteth, so will I comfort you; and ye shall be comforted in Jerusalem."
Isaiah 66:13 (KJV)

Loneliness cannot be reconciled by men or women; only God can satisfy us from the depths of our souls. He is everything that we need, and we must learn to desire God more than temporary satisfactions. When we constantly choose to satisfy our flesh, we become spiritually disconnected from the Father. Our battles were won on the cross, Jesus Christ overcame everything, and so can we!

Battling Develops Our Obedience

I returned and saw under the sun that, the race is not to the swift, Nor the battle to the strong, Nor bread to the wise, Nor riches to men of understanding, Nor favor to men of skill;
But time and chance happen to them all.
Ecclesiastes 9:11 (NKJV)

Everyone is tested; sometimes we pass and other times we fail [miserably]. We beat ourselves up because of our shortcomings, and sometimes we want to throw in the towel! Fortunately, the daily battles we face cultivate our obedience to God. The more obedient we are to God's will for our lives, the easier it is to trust Him. When we are obedient, we won't sacrifice our self-respect or self-worth. Obedience to God allows Him to move on our behalf in ways that exceed our ability to comprehend!

Battling Self-Destructive Behavior

"For God so loved the world, that he gave his only begotten Son, that whosoever believeth in him should not perish, but have everlasting life. For God sent not his Son into the world to condemn the world; but that the world through him might be saved." John 3:16-17 (KJV)

We are fallible, we mess up– it is inevitable! Consequently, not every unfortunate circumstance is a test or trial. Sometimes we are reaping a harvest or enduring the consequences of poor choices we made. We must examine ourselves and consider our actions before we cast blame outside of ourselves because many of us (myself included) have repeated the same dysfunctional cycles and expected a different result. This is ridiculous. We should learn from our shortcomings and others. Experience doesn't have to be the teacher you never wanted to have!

When we battle self-destructive behavior, we strengthen our faith in God. We also allow our hearts and minds to listen to the gentle nudging voice of the Holy Spirit. God loves us and He sent His son Jesus, so that no man would perish but have a blessed and abundant life!

Battling for Success & Achievement

"For the vision is yet for an appointed time, but at the end it shall speak, and not lie: though it tarry, wait for it; because it will surely come, it will not tarry."
Habakkuk 2:3 (KJV)

All things have an appointed time, including our dreams, ambitions, desires, and goals! The path to the success of these things is never straight. There is always a detour, or hindrance, or some unexpected calamity that knocks us off course. Naturally, we question if we are doing the right thing or if our efforts are even worth it?

When these questions creep into mind, the calming whisper of God's voice asks, "Do you trust me?" My answer is always, "Yes, Lord!" Ironically, deep down inside I usually feel uncertain. We don't know our future, but God established our destiny prior to our conception. We just have to trust Him; God always fulfills His purpose for our lives!

Battling is the Good Fight of Faith

So, fight with faith for the winner's prize! Lay your hands upon eternal life, for this is your calling—celebrating in faith before the multitude of witnesses!
1 Timothy 6:12 (TPT)
The Passion Translation

The struggle to live a victorious life that is pleasing to God, *daily,* is an emotional, mental, physical, and spiritual battle. However, the mere fact that we choose to struggle indicates that we love God more than our desire to fulfill selfish wants. God allows us to struggle because it is the *trying of our faith* and maturing us! Our faith must increase daily, for us to die daily to our desires.

Again, God does not expect us to be perfect, He desires us to be pure. However, He knows that we will falter. However, God desires that we lean on Him, trust in Him, follow him, and believe in Him. The daily battles we encounter are *"the good fight of faith"* and God delights in our willingness to depend on Him! So, we must continue fighting and we will not condemn ourselves because of our inevitable follies, but we will glorify the God of our salvation because we know He is our deliverer!

About the Author

Lynette Anderson is a God-lover, mother, rising gospel artist and worship leader. Since Lynette's childhood days of singing in her church's choir, she has had a deep and indescribable yearning to express her love for God through songs and worship.

Her latest project, *The Daily Battle Devotional,* highlights the honesty that God requires from us as we fight the battle of faith to live a victorious life.

Follow Lynette Anderson – artist and author – on social media.

CPSIA information can be obtained
at www.ICGtesting.com
Printed in the USA
LVHW090959070221
678443LV00020B/122